PIE POPS

PIE POPS

Miniature sweet and savory pies for all occasions

Carol Hilker

photography by Steve Painter

LONDON • NEW YORK

This book is dedicated to my biggest fan, my father Frank.

Design, photography and prop styling Steve Painter
Editor Ellen Parnavelas
Production Manager Gordana Simakovic
Art Director Leslie Harrington
Editorial Director Julia Charles

Indexer Hilary Bird
Food stylist Lucy McKelvie
Food stylist's assistant Ellie Jarvis

First published in 2013 by
Ryland Peters & Small
20–21 Jockey's Fields
London WC1R 4BW
and
519 Broadway, 5th Floor
New York, NY 10012
www.rylandpeters.com

10 9 8 7 6 5 4 3 2 1

Text © Carol Hilker 2013
Design and photographs
© Ryland Peters & Small 2013

ISBN: 978-1-84975-348-7

A CIP record for this book is available from the British Library.

US Library of Congress cataloging-in-Publication Data has been applied for

Printed in China

Notes:

* All spoon measurements are level, unless otherwise specified.

* Butter used in this book is unsalted, unless otherwise specified.

* Eggs used in this book are UK Medium, US Large.

* Ovens should be preheated to the specified temperatures. All ovens work slightly differently. We recommend using an oven thermometer and suggest you consult the maker's handbook for any special instructions, particularly if you are using a fan-assisted/convection oven, as you will need to adjust temperatures according to the manufacturer's instructions.

Author's Acknowledgments

Firstly, this book wouldn't exist at all without the hard work of the publishing, editorial and creative teams at Ryland Peters & Small, especially Julia Charles, Ellen Parnavelas, Steve Painter and Cindy Richards. Thank you all so much for this opportunity. I would also like to give a big thank you to my pie pop testers: Ashley Arteaga, Carol and Gus Arteaga and Brie Monks, Sophia and Justin Roof, Christina Smith, Steve and Patrice Yursik, Billy and Stephanie Condon, Joe and Nicole Bucci, Ian Tomele and Anthony Rubinas, who has tasted every one of these pie pops — some numerous times! I would also like to thank Marah Eakin for giving me a platform to write about food, and Theresa Rubinas for being an amazing help with all my projects. To my family, especially the Oregon clan, the Caron clan in Michigan, my brother, sister, nieces and nephews, Doreen and Larren Doniger and the entire Ruboneykillewicz family, thanks for everything always, I love you.

CONTENTS

06 **PRETTY AS PIE**

08 **FAVORITE PIES**

18 **FRUIT PIES**

34 **CHOCOLATE PIES**

44 **ICE CREAM PIES**

54 **SAVORY PIES**

64 **INDEX**

PRETTY AS PIE!

One of the many great things about pie is that it is consistent. It has always been around, and from the looks of things, it's not going anywhere. The pie has certainly evolved from its humble beginnings and has come a long way since it began as a food for basic sustenance. Pie making is now considered an art form in itself, with so many options for crumbly, flaky and comforting pastry and gooey fillings and whipped toppings available.

In this book, we have made miniature versions of a selection of best-loved pies to serve as pie pops on sticks. Pie pops are fun, delicious, bite-sized treats that require very little clean-up! Most of the pie pops in this book are made flat with either cake pop sticks or wooden ice lolly/popsicle sticks baked into them. However, some of the dessert pie pops are best served on upright pie pop holders. You can buy 'cake pop treat sticks' from baking suppliers or 'pastry pedestals' (www.pastrypedestal.com) or alternatively, here is a method you can follow to make simple platforms to mount your pretty pie pops on in order to display and serve them.

YOU WILL NEED:

a circular cookie cutter, at least 5-cm/2-inch diameter

a large cardboard cake board

cake pop sticks

a glue gun

Using the cookie cutter, draw out as many circles as you can fit on the cake board. Cut the circles out and poke a small, stick-sized hole in the middle of each. Push the cardboard circles about 1.5cm/½ inch down the stick and apply a little glue to the bottom of the cardboard circle to secure the bottom in place. Allow to dry. To mount the pies on the upright sticks, use the tip of a small, sharp knife and slowly carve a small hole, the size of a pop stick in the middle of the bottom of each of the pies. Put the pop stick into the hole in the bottom of the pie and ease the pie onto the stick, stopping before it goes all the way through the pie.

Tasty fillings and toppings aside, it pays to make your pies as pretty as possible – we've used a variety of novelty cookie cutters to achieve fun and interesting shapes. Why not visit www.cakescookiesandcraftsshop.co.uk and www.foosecookiecutters.com for a great choice of designs. And don't be afraid to try out your own pie pop design ideas – it's all part of the fun!

FAVORITE PIES

BUTTERSCOTCH PECAN PIE POPS

According to the French, it was they who made the first pie out of pecans after settling in New Orleans. Now a popular dessert in the American South, these miniature pie pops are a delicious variation on the classic recipe.

SHORTCRUST PASTRY:

280 g/2½ cups plain/all-purpose flour

2 tablespoons granulated sugar

1 teaspoon salt

230 g/2 sticks butter, chilled and diced

1 egg, beaten, mixed with 30 ml/ 2 tablespoons milk for egg wash

50 g/¼ cup brown sugar

PECAN FILLING:

90 g/½ cup brown soft sugar

a pinch of salt

60 g/½ stick butter, melted and cooled

1 egg

1 teaspoon vanilla extract

1 tablespoon Cognac (optional)

100 g/1 cup pecans, toasted

a 7.5-cm/3-inch round cookie cutter

a lattice pie roller

16 cake pop sticks

MAKES 16

To make the pastry, put the flour, granulated sugar and salt in a food processor and pulse to incorporate. Add the butter and mix on high for 10 seconds, or until the mixture resembles cornmeal. Pour 120 ml/½ cup ice-cold water into the mixture and combine again by pulsing the food processor for 20–30 seconds, until the mixture just starts to come together. It should be sticking together, not crumbly. Wrap the pastry with clingfilm/plastic wrap and chill in the fridge while you make the filling.

To make the filling, combine the brown sugar and salt together in a mixing bowl and stir in the melted butter, egg, vanilla extract and Cognac, if using. Chop the pecans and fold in.

Preheat the oven to 170 C (325 F) Gas 3.

Put the dough on a floured work surface. Break off two thirds and roll out to a 3-mm/⅛-inch thickness. Stamp out 16 rounds using the cookie cutter and lay on a baking sheet 2.5 cm/1 inch apart. Roll out the remaining pastry to the same thickness, and score with the lattice roller. Gently pull out the lattice-cut pastry to reveal the design and stamp out another 16 rounds using the cookie cutter. Coat the pastry rounds on the baking sheet with egg wash. Put a cake pop stick in the middle of each one, then add 2–3 teaspoonfuls of the pecan filling. Top with a lattice-cut pastry round and gently press around the edges to seal. Brush with egg wash, sprinkle with the brown sugar and bake in the middle of the preheated oven for 15–20 minutes, or until golden brown and the center puffs up. Take care when serving as the filling may be hot.

LEMON MERINGUE PIE POPS

Lemon-flavored custards, puddings and pies have been enjoyed since Medieval times, but meringue was not perfected until the 17th century. The earliest recorded recipe was attributed to a Swiss baker, and the recipe has stayed very authentic since. With their creamy citrus filling and dreamy meringue topping, these scrumptious pie pops won't disappoint!

1 quantity Shortcrust Pastry (p.8)

LEMON FILLING:

200 g/1 cup granulated sugar

2 tablespoons plain/all-purpose flour

2½ tablespoons cornflour/cornstarch

¼ teaspoon salt

freshly squeezed juice and zest of 3 unwaxed lemons

30 g/2 tablespoons butter

4 egg yolks, beaten

MERINGUE TOPPING:

4 egg whites

75 g/6 tablespoons granulated sugar

a 7.5-cm/3-inch round fluted cookie cutter

a 24-hole mini tartlet pan, greased

a piping bag

a chef's blow torch (optional)

24 upright pie pop holders (p.6)

MAKES 24

Preheat the oven to 180°C (350°F) Gas 4.

Put the pastry on a floured work surface and roll out to a 3-mm/⅛-inch thickness. Stamp out 24 pastry rounds using the cookie cutter and put back in the fridge to chill for 30 minutes. Prick the pastry rounds with a fork and fit them into the tartlet pan. Chill in the fridge for 5–10 minutes, then bake in the preheated oven for 25–30 minutes, or until golden and crisp. Set aside to cool.

To make the filling, whisk the sugar, flour, cornflour/cornstarch and salt together in a medium saucepan. Add 360 ml/1½ cups cold water and stir in the lemon juice and zest. Cook over medium–high heat, stirring frequently, until the mixture comes to a boil. Stir in the butter. Put the egg yolks in a heatproof bowl and gradually whisk in 120 ml/½ cup of the hot sugar mixture. Gradually add the rest of the mixture and combine well. Return to the saucepan and bring to the boil over medium heat, stirring constantly. Let simmer until the custard is thick and bubbling. Remove from the heat when the custard coats the spoon without dripping. Spoon or pour the filling into the baked pie shells. Set aside until needed.

To make the topping, beat the egg whites in a large, clean mixing bowl until foamy. Gradually pour in the sugar and beat until stiff peaks form. Spoon the mixture into a piping bag. Pipe a swirl of meringue on top of each filled tartlet. Lightly brown the meringue with a chef's blow torch or under a preheated grill/broiler. Carefully mount on upright pie pop holders to serve.

PUMPKIN PIE POPS

Pumpkin pie was first documented by American settlers as a native American dish. These cute jack-o-lantern pie pops are the perfect spooky treat to serve at any halloween party.

RICH SWEET PASTRY:

260 g/2½ cups plain/all-purpose flour

40 g/3 tablespoons granulated sugar

½ teaspoon salt

230 g/2 sticks butter, chilled and diced

1 large egg yolk, beaten

1 teaspoon vanilla extract

1 egg, beaten, mixed with 30 ml/ 2 tablespoons milk for egg wash

PUMPKIN FILLING:

140 g/¾ cup pumpkin purée

1 tablespoon pumpkin pie spice*

1 large egg

¼ teaspoon salt

75 ml/⅓ cup honey

a 7.5-cm/3-inch pumpkin-shaped cookie cutter

24 wooden ice lolly/popsicle sticks

MAKES 24

* If you can't buy pumpkin pie spice, make your own by blending 1 teaspoon ground cinnamon, ½ teaspoon ground ginger and ¼ teaspoon each ground nutmeg and allspice. Any not used can be stored in an airtight container.

To make the pastry, put the flour, sugar and salt in a food processor and pulse to incorporate. Add the butter and mix on high for 10 seconds, or until the mixture resembles cornmeal. Put the egg yolk in a bowl and pour in 60 ml/¼ cup ice-cold water. Add the vanilla extract and mix to combine. Add the egg mixture to the butter and flour and pulse in the food processor for 20–30 seconds, until the mixture just starts to come together. It should be sticking together, not crumbly. Wrap the pastry with clingfilm/plastic wrap and chill in the fridge while you make the filling.

To make the filling, heat the pumpkin purée and spice in a saucepan set over medium heat, just long enough for the spices to become fragrant. Remove from the heat and pour into a bowl to cool. When the filling comes to room temperature, whisk in the egg, salt and honey and chill in the fridge.

Put the pastry on a floured work surface and roll out to a 3-mm/⅛-inch thickness. Stamp out 48 pastry shapes using the cookie cutter. Use a sharp knife to cut out scary or fun faces from 24 of the shapes and put in the fridge to chill for about 30 minutes.

Preheat the oven to 180°C (350°F) Gas 4.

Take the pastry pumpkins from the fridge, coat with egg wash and lay on a baking sheet 2.5 cm/1 inch apart. Put a wooden stick in the middle of the plain pastry shapes, then add 1–2 tablespoons of pumpkin filling. Top each with a pastry shape with a cut-out face and seal the edges of the pies by crimping the pastry with a fork. Brush all the pies with egg wash. Bake in the middle of the preheated oven for 15–20 minutes, or until golden brown. Take care when serving as the filling may still be hot.

COCONUT CREAM PIE POPS

Coconut cream pie is one of the most popular custard pies there is. These mini versions team a vanilla pastry cream with toasted coconut in a chocolate shortbread pie crust.

CHOCOLATE PASTRY:

140 g/1¼ cups plain/all-purpose flour

65 g/⅓ cup granulated sugar

2 tablespoons unsweetened, Dutch process cocoa powder

¾ teaspoon salt

120 g/6 tablespoons butter, chilled

3 egg yolks, beaten

1½ teaspoons vanilla extract

VANILLA PASTRY CREAM:

320 ml/1⅓ cups whole milk

50 g/¼ cup granulated sugar

2 tablespoons cornflour/cornstarch

a pinch of salt

1 large egg

2 teaspoons vanilla extract

160 ml/⅔ cup double/heavy cream

1 teaspoon brown sugar

2 large handfuls of toasted coconut

TO FINISH:

450 ml/2 cups double/heavy cream, whipped

toasted coconut, to sprinkle

a 7.5-cm/3-inch round cookie cutter

a 24-hole mini tartlet pan, greased

24 upright pie pop holders (p.6)

MAKES 24

To make the pastry, put the flour, sugar, cocoa powder and salt in a food processor and pulse to incorporate. Add the butter and mix on high for 10 seconds, or until the mixture resembles cornmeal. Put the egg yolks in a bowl, add the vanilla extract and mix to combine. Add the egg mixture to the butter and flour and pulse in the food processor for 20–30 seconds, until the mixture just starts to come together. It should be sticking together, not crumbly. Wrap the pastry with clingfilm/plastic wrap and chill in the fridge while you make the filling.

To make the pastry cream, scald 240 ml/1 cup of milk over medium heat in a saucepan. Combine the granulated sugar, cornflour/cornstarch and salt in a heatproof bowl. Gradually whisk the remaining milk into the cornflour/cornstarch, a little at a time, then whisk in the egg. Once the milk is boiling, very gradually add it to the cornflour/cornstarch mixture in the bowl, whisking constantly. Return the mixture to the saucepan, stirring continuously. Simmer for 2 minutes, then stir in the vanilla extract and chill in the fridge until set.

Preheat the oven to 180°C (350°F) Gas 4.

Put the pastry on a floured work surface and roll out to a 3-mm/⅛-inch thickness. Stamp out 24 pastry rounds using the cookie cutter and put back in the fridge to chill for 5–10 minutes. Prick the pastry rounds with a fork and fit them into the tartlet pan. Chill in the fridge for 5–10 minutes, then bake in the oven for 25–30 minutes, or until crisp. Set aside to cool.

To finish the vanilla pastry cream, beat the cream and brown sugar together until soft peaks form and fold into the set pastry cream. Stir in the toasted coconut. Spoon into the cooled pie shells and top with whipped cream and toasted coconut. Carefully mount on upright pie pop holders to serve.

BANANA CREAM PIE POPS

Most home cooks know banana cream pie as a traditional treat that involves a vanilla custard spread into a pie shell and topped with heaps of sliced bananas, whipped cream and slivered almonds. This time-tested traditional pie has been a favorite for generation after generation. This recipe includes a traditional version of this pie, as well as an upgrade. By roasting the bananas in brown sugar and butter, it's a slight modification that goes a long way.

I quantity Vanilla Pastry Cream (p.15), omitting the coconut

I quantity Shortcrust Pastry (p.8)

CARAMELIZED BANANAS:

115 g/I stick butter

200 g/I cup brown sugar

I teaspoon salt

4 small bananas, sliced

TO FINISH:

450 ml/2 cups double/heavy cream, whipped

brown sugar, for sprinkling

a 7.5-cm/3-inch round fluted cookie cutter

24 x 6-cm/2½-inch mini fluted tartlet pans, greased

24 upright pie pop holders (p.6)

MAKES 24

Preheat the oven to 180°C (350°F) Gas 4.

Put the pastry on a floured work surface and roll out to a 3-mm/⅛-inch thickness. Stamp out 24 pastry rounds using the cookie cutter and put back in the fridge to chill for 5–10 minutes. Arrange the tartlet pans on a baking sheet. Prick the pastry rounds with a fork and fit them into the tartlet pans. Chill in the fridge for 5–10 minutes, then bake in the preheated oven for 25–30 minutes, or until golden and crisp. Set aside to cool.

To make the caramelized bananas, melt the butter in a saucepan over medium heat. Add the brown sugar and salt and turn the heat down to a medium–low. Cook until the mixture has become a thick melted caramel. Remove from the heat and fold the sliced bananas into the mixture. Stir to coat the bananas with the caramel sauce.

Spoon the vanilla pastry cream into the baked pie shells and carefully mount on upright pie pop holders. Once all the pies are assembled, top with as many caramelized bananas as the pie will hold, followed by a dollop of whipped cream, a slice of caramelized banana and a sprinkling of brown sugar.

FRUIT PIES

BLUEBERRY PIE POPS

The origin of blueberry pie goes back to the early American settlers, who have passed down heirloom blueberry pie recipes from generation to generation. In America, states like Michigan and Oregon are known for their abundance of blueberries; Maine adores the small, round, blue fruit so much that blueberry pie is the state's official dessert.

2 quantities Shortcrust Pastry (p.8)

1 egg, beaten, mixed with 30 ml/ 2 tablespoons milk for egg wash

granulated sugar, for sprinkling

BLUEBERRY FILLING:

500 g/4 cups fresh blueberries, washed and stems removed

1 teaspoon freshly squeezed lemon juice

3 tablespoons cornflour/ cornstarch

170 g/1½ cups granulated sugar

a pinch of salt

30 g/2 tablespoons very cold butter, diced

1 teaspoon finely grated lemon zest

a 7.5-cm/3-inch round cookie cutter

a round micro cookie cutter

24 cake pop sticks

MAKES 24

Put the pastry on a floured work surface and roll out to a 3-mm/⅛-inch thickness. Stamp out 48 pastry rounds using the larger cookie cutter. Stamp out 6 small holes (as shown) out of 24 of the rounds using the other cookie cutter. Put all of the rounds back in the fridge to chill for about 30 minutes.

To make the filling, put the blueberries and lemon juice in a small bowl and set aside for at least 20–30 minutes. Mix the cornflour/cornstarch, sugar and salt together in a separate bowl and add to the blueberries. Toss to fully incorporate. Add the butter to the mixture and set aside.

Preheat the oven to 190°C (375°F) Gas 5.

Take the pastry rounds from the fridge, coat with egg wash and lay out on a baking sheet 2.5 cm/1 inch apart. Put a cake pop stick in the middle of the plain pastry rounds, then add 1–2 tablespoons of the blueberry filling. Top each with a decorated pastry round and seal the edges of the pies by crimping the pastry with a fork. Brush all the pies with egg wash, sprinkle with sugar and bake in the middle of the preheated oven for 15–20 minutes, or until golden brown. If the filling is runny, turn off the oven when done and let them cool as the oven cools down. Take care when serving as the filling may be hot.

NECTARINE AND PEACH BROWN SUGAR PIE POPS

Known as a staple in the American South, peaches and nectarines are much celebrated in the US. Each summer, over thirty peach festivals take place, boasting pie contests, peach tastings and a menu of peach-related food that goes for miles. Keeping with the theme of the American south, these nectarine and peach pie pops use a shortbread crust infused with a little vanilla and take brown sugar and a little lemon to enhance the fruit, creating a filling of epic proportions.

2 quantities Rich Sweet Pastry (p.12)

1 egg, beaten, mixed with 30 ml/
2 tablespoons milk for egg wash

granulated sugar, for sprinkling

NECTARINE AND PEACH FILLING:

3 fresh peaches

2 fresh nectarines

1 teaspoon finely grated lemon zest

1 teaspoon freshly squeezed
lemon juice

¼ teaspoon ground cinnamon

a pinch of salt

40 g/3 tablespoons plain/
all-purpose flour

60 g/⅓ cup brown sugar

½ teaspoon vanilla extract

30 g/2 tablespoons butter, diced

a 7.5-cm/3-inch round cookie cutter

*a 7.5-cm/3-inch diameter flower-shaped
cookie cutter*

a 24-hole mini muffin pan, greased

24 upright pie pop holders (p.6)

MAKES 24

Put the pastry on a floured work surface and roll out to a 3-mm/⅛-inch thickness. Stamp out 24 pastry rounds and 24 pastry flowers using the cookie cutters and put the pastry flowers back in the fridge. Prick the pastry rounds with a fork and fit them into the muffin pan. Chill the pie shells and flowers in the fridge for 30 minutes.

To make the filling, peel and finely chop the peaches and nectarines and put in a large mixing bowl. Add the lemon zest and juice, cinnamon and salt and mix to combine. Set aside.

Mix the flour, brown sugar, vanilla and butter together in a food processor and process to crumbs. Add the peach and nectarine mixture and mix to combine.

Preheat the oven to 180°C (350°F) Gas 4.

Take the pie shells and pastry flowers from the fridge and spoon 1–2 tablespoons of filling into each pie shell. Top each pie with a pastry flower and seal the edges of the pies by pressing down at the tip of each flower petal. Poke a small hole in the middle of all the pies and brush with egg wash. Sprinkle with sugar and bake in the middle of the preheated oven for 15–20 minutes, or until golden brown. Carefully mount on upright pie pop holders to serve. Take care when serving as the filling may be hot.

STRAWBERRY POP TART POPS

In the early 1960s, the world was introduced to the first sealed pie that could be warmed and enjoyed fresh at any time of day — the Pop Tart. This strawberry recipe is an old classic and can be eaten plain as here or covered with icing and sprinkles, if you want it to be really authentic!

POP TART PASTRY:

240 g/2 cups plain/all-purpose flour plus extra for dusting

I tablespoon granulated sugar

I teaspoon salt

300 g/2 sticks plus 3½ tablespoons butter, diced

I large egg

2 tablespoons very cold milk

I egg, beaten, mixed with 30 ml/ 2 tablespoons milk for egg wash

STRAWBERRY FILLING:

450 g/I lb. fresh strawberries, hulled and sliced

600 g/3 cups granulated sugar

60 ml/¼ cup freshly squeezed lemon juice

2 tablespoons cornflour/ cornstarch mixed with 30 ml/ 2 tablespoons water

a crimped pastry wheel

24 wooden ice lolly/popsicle sticks

MAKES 20–24

To make the pastry, put the flour, sugar and salt in a food processor and pulse to incorporate. Add the butter and mix on high for 10 seconds, or until the mixture resembles cornmeal. Beat the egg and milk and add to the flour and butter mixture. Pulse in the food processor for 20–30 seconds, until the pastry just starts to come together. It should be sticking together, not crumbly. Divide into two balls and wrap with clingfilm/plastic wrap. Chill in the fridge while making the filling.

To make the filling, mash the strawberries in a bowl then put them in a saucepan with the sugar and lemon juice and stir over low heat until the sugar is dissolved. Increase the heat to high and bring to the boil. Set aside to cool. Once the mixture is cool, set over low heat, stir in half the cornflour/cornstarch mixture and simmer for 2 minutes. Turn the heat up to high and let boil for 1–3 minutes, just until the jam thickens and coats a spoon. If it isn't thickening, add the second half of the cornflour/cornstarch mixture and boil for 2 minutes more. When thickened, remove from the heat and let cool.

Preheat the oven to 180°C (350°F) Gas 4.

Remove the pastry from the fridge. Take one ball and roll it out until 3 mm/⅛ inches thick. (If you want a woven basket-effect finish as shown, roll the pastry out on a lightly-floured piece of textured paper or cloth.) Use a crimped pastry wheel to cut the pastry into 20–24 squares (each 8 cm/3 inches square), then chill in the fridge. Repeat with the remaining pastry. Lay out the pastry squares on greased baking sheets. Brush with egg wash. Put a wooden stick in the middle of half of them and top with 1½ teaspoons of strawberry filling, about 1.5 cm/½ inch from the edges. Place a pastry square on top and seal. Bake in the preheated oven for 15 minutes, or until golden. Take care when serving as the filling will be hot.

SHAKER LEMON PIE POPS

The shaker lemon pie originated in Ohio. The Shakers were a religious group who had chapters everywhere from Ohio to Maine during the mid-1800s and were notorious for penny pinching. Thrifty to the point of not wanting to waste even the smallest piece of lemon peel — they made this pie that incorporates the whole lemon, with surprisingly delicious results!

2 quantities Shortcrust Pastry (p.8)

I egg, beaten, mixed with 30 ml/
2 tablespoons milk for egg wash

24 raisins, to decorate (optional)

LEMON FILLING:

2 Meyer lemons, washed with skin
left on, very thinly sliced

400 g/2 cups granulated sugar

4 eggs

¼ teaspoon salt

I teaspoon vanilla extract

a 6.5-cm/2½-inch lemon-shaped cookie cutter

24 ice lolly/popsicle sticks

a cocktail stick/toothpick

MAKES 24

Before making the pastry, toss the lemons for the filling with the sugar in a mixing bowl and let sit for at least 3 hours, but no more than overnight.

Put the pastry on a floured work surface and roll out to a 3-mm/⅛-inch thickness. Stamp out 48 pastry shapes using the cookie cutter and put back in the fridge to chill.

To make the lemon filling, lightly whisk the eggs, salt and vanilla together in a mixing bowl and add the lemon mixture. Mix well to incorporate.

Preheat the oven to 180°C (350°F) Gas 4.

Take the pastry shapes from the fridge, coat with egg wash and lay on a baking sheet 2.5 cm/1 inch apart. Put a wooden stick in the middle of half of the pastry shapes, then add 1–2 tablespoons of the filling. Top each with another pastry shape and seal the edges of the pies. Prick holes all over the tops of the pies with a cocktail stick/toothpick and brush them with egg wash.

Decorate each pie with a raisin to make the stalks of the lemons, if using, and bake in the middle of the preheated oven for 15–20 minutes, or until golden brown. Take care when serving as the filling may be hot.

CHERRY PIE POPS

Cherry Pie Day is traditionally celebrated on February 20th in the US in homage to America's first President, George Washington. Washington is famous for saying the words, "I cannot tell a lie, I chopped down the cherry tree." In honor of Washington's birthday, it is a tradition to bake a pie on this day to celebrate Cherry Pie Day.

2 quantities Shortcrust Pastry (p.8)

I egg, beaten, mixed with 30 ml/ 2 tablespoons milk for egg wash

granulated sugar, for sprinkling

CHERRY FILLING:

4 tablespoons quick-cooking tapioca

a pinch of salt

200 g/1 cup granulated sugar

580 g/4 cups pitted cherries

½ teaspoon almond extract

¼ teaspoon vanilla extract

I tablespoon Kirsch (optional)

20 g/1½ tablespoons butter, diced

a 7.5-cm/3-inch fluted round cookie cutter

a heart-shaped micro cookie cutter (optional)

24 cake pop sticks

MAKES 24

Put the pastry on a floured work surface and roll out to a 3-mm/⅛-inch thickness. Stamp out 48 pastry rounds using the cookie cutter and put in the fridge to chill.

To make the cherry filling, combine the tapioca, salt, sugar, cherries, almond extract, vanilla extract and Kirsch, if using, in a large bowl. Let sit for 15 minutes. Mix and add the butter to the mixture. Mix again.

Preheat the oven to 190°C (375°F) Gas 5.

Take the pastry rounds from the fridge, coat with egg wash and lay on a baking sheet 2.5 cm/1 inch apart. Put a cake pop stick in the middle of half of the pastry rounds, then add 1–2 tablespoons of the cherry filling. Stamp out 3 small heart-shaped holes (as shown) in the top of the remaining pastry rounds or simply cut a few small slits with a sharp knife. Use these to top each filled pie half and seal the edges of the pies by gently pinching the pastry. Brush all the pies with egg wash. Sprinkle with sugar and bake in the middle of the preheated oven for 30 minutes, or until golden brown. If the filling is runny, turn off the oven when done and let them cool as the oven cools down. Take care when serving as the filling may still be hot.

APPLE PIE POPS

Although Americans claim it as their own, the apple pie dates back to 14th-century England. Other early versions of the famous pie included Dutch apple pies, which used lemon juice and cinnamon and a variety of toppings. The Swedish version of the apple pie is more like a baked apple cake without a pastry crust. This recipe takes apples at their finest and adds a dash of ginger and cinnamon to make a sweet, delicately spiced apple pie pop.

2 quantities Shortcrust Pastry (p.8)

I egg, beaten, mixed with 30 ml/ 2 tablespoons milk for egg wash

APPLE FILLING:

5 medium Granny Smith or Pink Lady apples, peeled, cored and thickly sliced

a squeeze of lemon juice

140 g/⅔ cup granulated sugar

2 teaspoons ground cinnamon

I teaspoon ground ginger

a 6-cm/2½-inch apple-shaped cookie cutter

24 cake pop sticks

MAKES 24

For the filling, put the apples in a large bowl of water mixed with a squeeze of lemon juice and set aside until ready to use.

Put the pastry on a floured work surface and roll out to a 3-mm/ ⅛-inch thickness. Stamp out 48 pastry shapes using the cookie cutter and put back in the fridge to chill for 30 minutes.

Preheat the oven to 180°C (350°F) Gas 4.

To make the apple filling, put the sugar, cinnamon and ginger in a bowl and mix to combine. Drain the apples and add the cinnamon mixture. Mix together until the cinnamon mixture is evenly distributed.

Take the pastry shapes from the fridge, coat with egg wash and lay on a baking sheet 2.5 cm/I inch apart. Put a cake pop stick in the middle of half of the pastry shapess, then add I–2 tablespoons of the apple filling. Top each with another pastry shape and prick around the edges with a fork to seal the pies. Brush all the pies with egg wash and bake in the middle of the preheated oven for 15–20 minutes, or until golden brown. Take care when serving as the filling will be hot.

APPLE AND BRIE TURNOVER POPS

These baked apple and brie treats mix the sweet with the savory. Puff pastry encloses a big slice of bubbly brie and apples baked in brown sugar, butter and salt. To tie the flavors together, a dollop of fruit jam is also baked inside the puff pastry triangle. These are quick, delicious and are a perfect go-to treat for anyone. For those who prefer a more savory flavor, use less sugar. For those who prefer more sweet, sprinkle sugar on top before baking and dip in melted jam.

500 g/1 lb. 2 oz. ready-made puff pastry, defrosted and brought to room temperature, if frozen

1 egg yolk, combined with 15 ml/ 1 tablespoon water for egg wash

225 g/8 oz. brie, rind removed and cut into 1-cm/½-inch pieces

APPLE FILLING:

30 g/2 tablespoons butter, diced

100 g/½ cup granulated sugar mixed with 50 g/¼ cup brown sugar

1 teaspoon ground cinnamon

¼ teaspoon salt

1 teaspoon vanilla extract

4 large Granny Smith apples, peeled, cored and cut into small pieces

100 g/⅓ cup apricot jam or jelly

20 cake pop sticks

MAKES 20

Preheat the oven to 200°C (400°F) Gas 6.

To make the filling, melt the butter in a saucepan set over medium heat and add the sugar, cinnamon and salt. Cook until the sugar has melted into a caramel, then add the vanilla. Add the apples and cook for about 3 minutes, or until the apples start to soften just a little. Set aside to cool.

Unfold the puff pastry sheet onto a lightly floured surface. Roll out to a 38 x 30-cm/15 x 12-inch rectangle and cut into 20 x 7.5-cm/3-inch squares. Apply a thin coat of egg wash across the whole of each pastry square, turn on its point and put a cake pop stick in the middle of each one. Put 1 teaspoon of jam on the right-hand side of each pastry square. Top with a slice of brie and 1–2 teaspoons of the apple filling. Fold the left-hand side over the right-hand side to make a triangle and press down with the tines of a fork to seal tightly.

Brush the tops with egg wash and bake in the preheated oven for 15–20 minutes, until the brie is melted. Let cool a little and serve. Take care when serving as the filling may still be hot.

MINI TARTE TATIN POPS

According to legend, the Tarte Tatin was created in France in the 1880s by two sisters, Stephanie and Caroline Tatin. Stephanie Tatin left the apples, butter and sugar on the stove too long one day when making an apple pie. Trying to quickly fix the pie, she threw a piece of pastry on top and put it in the oven. The guests loved it and the rest, as they say, is history…

500 g/1 lb. 2 oz. ready-made puff pastry, thawed and brought to room temperature, if frozen

sweetened whipped cream, to serve

CARAMELIZED APPLES:

6 Golden Delicious, Pippin or Royal Gala apples, peeled, cored and quartered

2½ teaspoons freshly squeezed lemon juice

100 g/½ cup vanilla sugar

30 g/2 tablespoons butter, diced

a 7.5 cm/3-inch round cookie cutter

a 24-hole mini tartlet or muffin pan

a baking sheet, lined with parchment paper

24 upright pie pop holders (p.6)

MAKES 20–24

To make the caramelized apples, put the apples in a large bowl, add 2 teaspoons of lemon juice and half of the vanilla sugar and mix to combine.

Put the remaining vanilla sugar and 2 tablespoons of water in a heavy frying pan/skillet over low heat, stirring constantly to dissolve the sugar. Once the sugar has dissolved, increase the heat to medium and cook for about 5 minutes until the sugar is caramelized to a light golden brown. Do not stir at this time but swish the pan to incorporate. Add ½ teaspoon of lemon juice and give the caramel a swish – this will stop the caramel from burning or overcooking. Add the apples, and the butter and mix to incorporate. Keeping the heat very low, cook for a further 5–6 minutes just to partially cook the apples. Remove from the heat and set aside to cool.

Preheat the oven to 180°C (350°F) Gas 4.

Unfold the puff pastry sheet onto a lightly floured surface and stamp or cut out 20–24 rounds using the cookie cutter – these need to be just slightly larger than the holes in the tartlet pans. Evenly distribute the caramelized apple in the holes in the tartlet pan, filling them three quarters full. Put the pastry rounds over the apples, tucking any excess underneath. Bake in the preheated oven for 30–35 minutes, or until the pastry is cooked and golden. Remove from the oven and allow to rest in the pan for 10 minutes. When cool enough to handle, carefully turn the pan upside down onto a baking sheet lined with parchment paper. Poke holes in the bottom of each tartlet with the tip of a sharp knife and rotate until a small hole forms. Carefully mount the tatins on the upright pie pop sticks and serve warm with sweetened whipped cream.

CHOCOLATE PIES

BOSTON CREAM PIE POPS

Created by an Armenian-French chef at Boston's Parker House Hotel in 1856, the Boston Cream Pie is considered one of America's most traditional desserts. In this New England classic, vanilla pastry cream is dolloped inside a miniature cupcake that has been sliced in half. The pie is then topped with melted chocolate, whipped cream and finished with a cherry on top.

1 quantity Vanilla Pastry Cream (p.15), omitting the coconut

CAKE BATTER:

120 g/1 cup plain/all-purpose flour

2 tablespoons plus 2 teaspoons cornflour/cornstarch

1 teaspoon baking powder

¼ teaspoon salt

115 g/1 stick butter, at room temperature and cubed

150 g/¾ cup granulated sugar

4 egg yolks

1 teaspoon vanilla extract

5 tablespoons milk

TO FINISH:

175 g/1 cup dark/semi-sweet chocolate chips

450 ml/2 cups double/heavy cream, whipped

24 black cherries, fresh or canned

a 24 hole mini cupcake pan, greased

a piping bag fitted with a star-shaped nozzle

24 upright pie pop holders (p.6)

MAKES 24

Preheat oven to 180°C (350°F) Gas 4.

To make the cake batter, sift the flour, cornflour/cornstarch, baking powder and salt together twice and set aside. Cream the butter and sugar together in a large bowl until the sugar is dissolved and the mixture is pale yellow and fluffy. Add the egg yolks, one at a time, beating on high with a hand-held whisk for 5 seconds each time to incorporate. Stir in the vanilla extract.

Add 40 g/⅓ cup of the flour mixture to the egg and sugar mixture and stir to incorporate, then stir in 2 tablespoons of milk. Do not beat or over-mix, the mixture should be just incorporated. Repeat until all the egg mixture and milk are used up. Fill each hole of the mini cupcake pan three quarters full of cake batter. Bake the pies in the preheated oven for 12 minutes, or until the tops spring back when lightly tapped (rotating the pan halfway through cooking). Remove from the oven and allow to cool for 15 minutes before turning out onto a wire rack.

When cooled, cut the cakes in half horizontally. Put 2 teaspoons of vanilla pastry cream onto the bottom half of each cake and top with the remaining halves. Put the filled cakes in the fridge to firm.

Meanwhile, put the chocolate chips in a heatproof bowl set over a saucepan of barely simmering water. Do not let the base of the bowl touch the water. When the chocolate is melted, remove it from the heat and use 1 teaspoon of it to cover the tops of each assembled pie. Return the pies to the fridge to set the chocolate.

When the chocolate has set, mount the pies on upright pie holders, spoon the whipped cream into a piping bag and pipe a swirl of cream on top of each pie. Top with a cherry to serve.

CHOCOLATE AND PEANUT BUTTER PIE POPS

H.B. Reese's candy company first brought the winning flavor combination of peanut butter and chocolate to our attention in the 1920s and it has been used to make scrumptious confectionery ever since. Make these delicious pie pops even more indulgent by finishing them with a creamy chocolate coating.

1 quantity Chocolate Pastry (p.15)
225 g/1½ cups smooth peanut butter
1 egg, beaten, mixed with 30 ml/ 2 tablespoons milk for egg wash
175 g/1 cup milk/semi-sweet chocolate chips, melted (p.35), to decorate

a 6-cm/2½-inch round cookie cutter
a patterned pastry stamp (optional)
a baking sheet, lined with parchment paper
24 cake pop sticks

MAKES 24

Preheat the oven to 180°C (350°F) Gas 4.

Put the pastry on a floured work surface and roll out to a 3-mm/⅛-inch thickness. Stamp out 48 pastry rounds using the cookie cutter and press with a patterned pastry stamp, if liked. Put back in the fridge to chill for 5–10 minutes.

Take the pastry rounds from the fridge, coat with egg wash and lay on a baking sheet 2.5 cm/1 inch apart. Put a cake pop stick in the middle of half of the pastry rounds, then add 1–2 tablespoons of peanut butter. Top each with another pastry round and press gently to seal the edges of the pies. Cut small slits in the pies and bake in the middle of the preheated oven for 30–40 minutes. Remove from the oven and allow to cool completely before finishing.

To finish, partially dip the pies into the melted chocolate and lay on a baking sheet covered with parchment paper. Leave to set completely before serving.

CHOCOLATE PUDDING PIE POPS

What could be better than golden, flaky pastry filled with delicious chocolate custard? Pair this pie pop with whipped cream or vanilla ice cream and you have a treat that reinvents the legendary chocolate pudding pie that has graced many a cafeteria with its chocolatey goodness.

1 quantity Shortcrust Pastry (p.8)

1 egg, beaten, mixed with 30 ml/ 2 tablespoons milk for egg wash

granulated sugar, for sprinkling

whipped cream or vanilla ice cream, to serve

CHOCOLATE FILLING:

120 ml/½ cup milk

120 ml/½ cup double/heavy cream

120 g/⅔ cup milk/semi-sweet chocolate, chopped

50 g/¼ cup granulated sugar

1 teaspoon cornflour/cornstarch

1 teaspoon vanilla extract

a 7.5-cm/3-inch round cookie cutter

a patterned pastry stamp (optional)

24 cake pop sticks

MAKES 24

Put the pastry on a floured work surface and roll out to a 3-mm/⅛-inch thickness. Stamp out 24 pastry rounds using the cookie cutter and press with a patterned pastry stamp, if using. Put back in the fridge to chill for 5–10 minutes.

To make the chocolate filling, put the milk, cream, chocolate, sugar and cornflour/cornstarch and vanilla extract in a saucepan set over low–medium heat. Stir the mixture continuously using a balloon whisk, until it thickens and comes to a simmer. Simmer for 30 seconds. The mixture should be thick. Remove from the heat, transfer to a bowl, cover and chill in the fridge. As it cools, it will thicken.

Preheat the oven to 180°C (350°F) Gas 4.

Take the pastry rounds from the fridge, coat with egg wash and lay on a greased baking sheet 2.5–5 cm/1–2 inches apart. Put a cake pop stick in the middle of each pastry round, then put 1–2 tablespoons of the chocolate filling onto the right-hand half of each pastry round. Fold the pastry in the middle and bring the left-hand half of each pastry round over the right to form a semi-circle. Press gently to seal the edges of the pies. Brush all the pies with egg wash, sprinkle with sugar and bake in the middle of the preheated oven for 30 minutes, or until golden brown. Serve with a small dish of whipped cream or vanilla ice cream on the side.

CARAMEL MARSHMALLOW PIE POPS

These caramel marshmallow pie pops are reminiscent of traditional toasted S'mores with a gooey layer of caramel in the middle. For a quick fix, home bakers can use store-bought caramels and marshmallows but they are even better if you make them yourself. Decorate with chocolate frosting and multi-colored sprinkles for an extra special treat!

1 quantity Pop Tart Pastry (p.23)

S'MORE FILLING:

40 mini marshmallows

20 pieces of soft caramel or toffee, chilled in the freezer

CHOCOLATE FROSTING:

50 g/¼ cup margarine, melted

50 g/½ cup unsweetened cocoa powder

80 ml/⅓ cup milk

1 teaspoon vanilla extract

350 g/3½ cups icing/confectioners' sugar

a 7.5-cm/3-inch birdhouse-shaped cookie cutter, or similar

a mini heart-shaped cookie cutter

24 cake pop sticks

MAKES 20

Put the pastry on a floured work surface and roll out to a 3-mm/⅛-inch thickness. Stamp out 40 shapes using the cookie cutter. Stamp out a small heart shapes in 20 of them and put back in the fridge to chill for 30 minutes.

Preheat the oven to 180°C (350°F) Gas 4.

Take the pastry shapes from the fridge, coat with egg wash and lay on a baking sheet 2.5 cm/1 inch apart. Put a cake pop stick in the middle of the shapes without the stamped out heart. Put 2 marshmallows and 1 piece of caramel on top of each pop stick, leaving a border of about 1.5 cm/½ inch. Top each with one of the remaining pastry shapes and press gently to seal the edges of the pies. Brush all the pies with egg wash. Bake in the middle of the preheated oven for 30 minutes, or until golden brown.

To make the chocolate frosting, beat the margarine and cocoa together in a large bowl until combined. Add the milk and vanilla extract and beat until smooth. Beat in the icing/confectioners' sugar until the desired consistency is achieved. Add more milk or icing/confectioners' sugar as needed.

Paint chocolate frosting around the heart-shaped hole in the middle of each pie pop and finish with sugar sprinkles. Let the frosting set before serving.

CHOCOLATE TURTLE PIE POPS

This chocolate pie is inspired by the delicious chocolate and caramel turtle candy. Caramel lines the bottom of a slightly salty shortcrust pastry base. Chocolate filling and pecans are added on top and it is finished with a generous coating of melted chocolate, creating a pie that is even more delicious than the candy itself.

I quantity Chocolate Pastry (p.15)

CARAMEL FILLING:

12 pieces of caramel or toffee

1 x 400-ml/14-oz. can of sweetened condensed milk

CHOCOLATE FILLING:

50 g/2 oz. dark/semi-sweet chocolate

60 g/4 tablespoons butter

2 eggs

½ tablespoon vanilla extract

a pinch of salt

100 g/¾ cup pecans, chopped

TO FINISH:

175 g/1 cup milk/semi-sweet chocolate chips, melted (p.35)

white chocolate sprinkles and star-shaped sprinkles, to decorate

a 7.5-cm/3-inch round cookie cutter

a 24-hole mini muffin pan, well greased

a baking sheet, lined with parchment paper

24 wooden ice lolly/popsicle sticks

MAKES 24

Preheat the oven to 180°C(350°F) Gas 4.

Put the pastry on a floured work surface and roll out to a 3-mm/⅛-inch thickness. Stamp out 24 pastry rounds using the cookie cutter. Prick them with a fork and fit them into the muffin pan. Chill in the fridge for 5–10 minutes, then bake for 25–30 minutes, or until golden and crisp. Set aside to cool. Reduce the oven temperature to 160°C (325°F) Gas 3.

To make the caramel filling, mix the caramels or toffees with 90 ml/⅓ cup of the condensed milk in a saucepan set over medium heat, whisking continuously until the caramels melt and the mixture is smooth. Spread the caramel mixture on the bottom of the baked pie shells, distributing evenly.

To make the chocolate filling, melt the chocolate and butter in a small saucepan set over low heat. Mix until smooth. Remove from the heat and set aside to cool. Beat the remaining condensed milk, eggs, 2 tablespoons of water, vanilla and salt together in a mixing bowl. Pour the chocolate mixture slowly into the milk and egg mixture, beating well to mix. Spoon the chocolate filling into the caramel-filled pie shells and then top with ¼–½ teaspoon of pecans. Bake in the preheated oven for 10–12 minutes, until the middles are puffy. Remove from the oven and allow to cool to room temperature before turning out onto the lined baking sheet.

Cut a small slit in the base of each pie with a sharp knife and insert a wooden stick. Dip each pie in the melted chocolate to coat and dust with sprinkles and return it to the baking sheet. Repeat until all the pies have been decorated. Transfer to the fridge for 2 hours to set before serving.

ICE CREAM PIES

CHOCOLATE-DIPPED KEY LIME PIE POPS

Key lime pie is named after the small key limes that produce a juice light yellow in color and grow most prominently in the Florida Keys. These tangy, chocolate-covered frozen treats are the perfect sweet bite to enjoy on a hot summer's day.

GRAHAM CRACKER PIE CRUST:

150 g/1½ cups finely crushed digestive biscuits/graham crackers

65 g/⅓ cup granulated sugar

85 g/6 tablespoons butter, melted

½ teaspoon ground cinnamon

KEY LIME FILLING:

5 egg yolks

240 ml/1 cup freshly squeezed lime juice (Key limes if available)

2 x 400-ml/14-oz. cans sweetened condensed milk

2 tablespoons finely grated lime zest (Key limes if available)

175 g/1 cup milk/semi-sweet chocolate chips, melted (p.35)

a 20-cm/8-inch disposable foil pie pan

a 5-cm/2-inch heart-shaped cookie cutter

8–10 wooden ice lolly/popsicle sticks

a baking sheet, lined with parchment paper

MAKES 8–10

Preheat the oven to 190°C (375°F) Gas 5.

To make the pie crust, mix the biscuit/cracker crumbs, sugar, butter and cinnamon until combined. Press the mixture into the disposable pie pan and bake in the preheated oven for 7–9 minutes. Let cool then transfer to the freezer for 1 hour.

To make the Key lime filling, beat the egg yolks in a heatproof bowl. Add the lime juice and whisk to combine. Set the bowl over a pan of simmering water (making sure the base of the bowl does not touch the water) and whisk continuously until the mixture is foamy and smooth. Remove the bowl from the heat, whisk in the condensed milk and stir in the lime zest. Pour the filling into the frozen pie crust and level the top with a spatula. Freeze for at least 1 hour.

Remove the pan from the freezer. Using a heart-shaped cookie cutter, score 8–10 shapes, with the bottom of the heart closest to the edge of the foil pan. Make a small horizontal slit in the bottom of each heart shape by poking the tip of a very sharp knife through the foil from the outside of the pan. Slowly insert a wooden stick into the middle of each slit. Cover the pan and return it to the freezer for at least 4 hours.

To remove the pies from the pan, use scissors or a knife to carefully cut down the side of the pan towards each stick and peel the foil away from the pie. Cut the pie into its pre-scored heart-shaped pieces (either with the cookie cutter or a sharp knife) and return the frozen shapes to the freezer while you melt the chocolate. Dip each pie in melted chocolate to coat and put on a lined baking sheet. Return to the freezer to set before serving.

CHOCOLATE CHERRY CHEESECAKE PIE POPS

The cheesecake dates back over 4,000 years to ancient Greece where a cheesecake made with honey, flour, wheat and cheese was served as wedding cake, and also enjoyed by athletes during the first Olympic games in 776 BC. Marcus Cato, a Roman politician in the first century BC, is the author of the first known cheesecake recipe, and it was modified repeatedly in Europe before being brought over to America.

1 quantity Graham Cracker Pie Crust mixture (p.44)

CHEESECAKE FILLING:

100 g/½ cup granulated sugar

2 x 225-g/8-oz packages of cream cheese, softened to room temperature

2 eggs

¾ teaspoon vanilla extract

450 g/2 cups stoned morello cherries (drained of syrup), either canned or bottled

TO FINISH:

175 g/1 cup milk/semi-sweet chocolate chips, melted (p.35) and cooled

a large handful of biscuit/cracker crumbs, to sprinkle

a 20-cm/8-inch disposable foil pie pan

8 wooden ice lolly/popsicle sticks

MAKES 8

Preheat the oven to 170°C (325°F) Gas 3.

To make the pie crust, press the mixture into a disposable pie pan and bake for 7–9 minutes. Let cool.

To make the cheesecake filling, beat the sugar and cream cheese with a hand-held mixer on medium–high speed for 8–10 minutes, until smooth. Stir in the eggs and vanilla extract until just combined. Mix in the cherries. Pour the filling into the pie crust and bake in the preheated oven for about 35 minutes. Remove from the oven and transfer to the fridge to set.

Score the top of the pie into 8 slices of equal size with a sharp knife. Make a small horizontal slit in each slice of pie by poking the tip of the knife into each one from the outside of the pan. Slowly insert a wooden stick into each slit. Cover the pan and transfer to the freezer for at least 4 hours. Remove from the freezer and spoon over the cooled melted chocolate, scatter over the biscuit/cracker crumbs and return to the freezer.

To remove the pie slices from the pan, use scissors or a knife to carefully cut down the side of the pan towards each stick and peel the foil away. Cut the pie into 8 slices. Return them to the freezer until ready to serve.

SUNDAE ALASKA PIE POPS

These pie pops are a new take on the Baked Alaska. They combine lemon sorbet with strawberry ice cream and are topped with baked meringues to create layers of flavor and texture.

1 quantity Shortcrust Pastry (p.8)

1 quantity Meringue Topping (p.11)

LEMON SORBET:

150 g/¾ cup granulated sugar

175 ml/¾ cup freshly squeezed lemon juice

2 teaspoons finely grated lemon zest

STRAWBERRY ICE CREAM:

240 ml/1 cup heavy/double whipping cream

120 ml/½ cup whole milk

2 large egg yolks (reserve the whites for the meringue topping)

50 g/¼ cup granulated sugar

a pinch of salt

1 teaspoon vanilla extract

240 ml/1 cup strawberry purée or sauce

an ice cream maker

a 7.5-cm/3-inch round fluted cookie cutter

a 24-hole mini muffin pan, greased

a piping bag

a chef's blow torch (optional)

24 upright pie pop holders (p.6)

MAKES 24

To make the lemon sorbet, put the sugar in a saucepan with 350 ml/1½ cups water and set over medium–high heat. Boil for 5 minutes, stirring continuously and set aside to cool. Add the lemon juice and zest. Pour into an ice cream maker and freeze according to the manufacturer's instructions.

To make the strawberry ice cream, put the cream and milk in a saucepan and set over medium heat. Cook until scalding then set aside. Beat the egg yolks, sugar and salt together in a heatproof bowl. Slowly whisk the hot milk into the egg mixture. After more than half has been incorporated, pour the rest in and whisk quickly. Return to the saucepan and cook over low heat, stirring continuously, until the mixture coats the back of a wooden spoon. Remove from the heat and let cool to room temperature, whisking often. Stir in the vanilla extract then chill in the fridge. When well chilled, mix in half of the strawberry sauce and pour into an ice cream maker. Freeze according to the manufacturer's instructions.

Preheat the oven to 180°C (350°F) Gas 4. Put the pastry on a floured work surface and roll out to a 3-mm/⅛-inch thickness. Stamp out 24 pastry rounds using the cookie cutter. Fit them into the muffin pan, prick with a fork and chill in the fridge for 5–10 minutes. Bake in the preheated oven for 25–30 minutes, until golden and crisp. Set aside to cool completely before assembling.

When ready to assemble, put 1 teaspoon of ice cream into the bottom of each cooled pie shell. Cover with 1 teaspoon of the reserved strawberry purée then return to the freezer for 10–20 minutes. Top each pie with 1 teaspoon of sorbet and pipe a swirl of meringue on top. Lightly brown the meringue with a chef's blow torch or under a preheated grill/broiler. Mount on upright pie pop holders and serve immediately.

ORANGESICLE ICE CREAM PIE POPS

Throughout the 20th century, there were several desserts that combined oranges and cream, but never was one as successful as the orangesicle ice cream bar. Combining orange juice and a creamy mixture of sour cream and cream, this play on a childhood treat is all grown up.

1 quantity Shortcrust Pastry (p.8)

ORANGESICLE ICE CREAM:

130 g /1/2–2/3 cup granulated sugar

4 tablespoons freshly grated
orange zest

310 ml/1¼ cups orange soda pop
(such as Fanta) or orange juice

240 g/1 cup sour cream

125 ml/½ cup double/heavy cream

TO FINISH:

175 g/1 cup dark/semi-sweet
chocolate chips, melted (p.35)

orange sanding sugar, to decorate

*24 x 5-cm/2-inch loose-bottomed mini
tartlet pans, greased*

a 7.5-cm/3-inch round fluted cookie cutter

a baking sheet, lined with parchment paper

24 wooden ice lolly/popsicle sticks

MAKES 24

To make the ice cream, put the sugar and orange zest in a blender and blend until the zest is very fine. Add the orange soda or juice, sour cream and cream and blend until the sugar is completely dissolved. Transfer to a bowl, cover and chill the mixture thoroughly in the fridge.

Preheat the oven to 180°C (350°F) Gas 4.

Arrange the tartlet pans on a baking sheet. Put the pastry on a floured work surface and roll out to a 3-mm/⅛-inch thickness. Stamp out 24 pastry rounds using the cookie cutter and fit them into the tartlet pans. Prick the pastry rounds with a fork then chill in the fridge for 5–10 minutes. Bake in the preheated oven for 25–30 minutes, or until golden and crisp. Set aside to cool.

Spoon 1–2 tablespoons of the orange mixture into the cooled pie shells. Put the pies back in the freezer and allow to freeze for at least 8 hours, ideally overnight. Remove the tartlet pans from the freezer. When firm, carefully turn the pies out onto a lined baking sheet. Make a small horizontal slit in the pastry of each pie with the tip of a sharp knife. Slowly insert a wooden stick into each one.

To finish, dip the frozen pies in melted dark/semi-sweet chocolate, sprinkle with orange sanding sugar and return to the freezer to set the chocolate completely before serving.

BANANA-SPLIT ICE CREAM PIE POPS

This soda fountain classic was invented in 1904 in Pennsylvania. Over 100 years later, the ice cream treat is still a popular commodity at ice cream parlors all over the world. This pie pop combines all the goodies that go together to make a perfect banana split on a stick.

1 quantity Chocolate Pastry (p.15)

ICE CREAM:

280 g/10 oz. fresh strawberries

200 g/1 cup granulated sugar

1 tablespoon plus 1½ teaspoons plain/all-purpose flour

¼ teaspoon salt

470 ml/2 cups whole milk

175 ml/¾ cup evaporated milk

3 eggs

2 teaspoons vanilla extract

500 ml/2 cups chocolate milk

2 bananas, diced, plus extra pieces to garnish

200 ml/¾ cup crushed pineapple

TO FINISH:

175 g/6 oz. dark/semi-sweet chocolate chips, melted (p.35)

whipped cream

24 pieces of glacé/candied cherry

chopped toasted nuts

an ice cream maker

a 7.5-cm/3-inch cookie cutter

a piping bag, fitted with a star-shaped nozzle

a 24-hole fluted mini tartlet pan, greased

24 upright pie pop holders (p.6)

MAKES 24

To make the ice cream, hull the strawberries, cut them into pieces and freeze them while you make the rest of the ice cream. Put the sugar, flour, salt, milk and evaporated milk in a saucepan set over medium heat. Heat until the mixture is slightly thickened and bubbles form along the edge of the saucepan. Break the eggs into a heatproof bowl and beat. Using 125 ml/¼ cup at a time, pour the hot milk mixture into the eggs and stir furiously. Continue until the egg and the milk mixture is combined and then transfer to an ice bath to cool. Once cool, stir in the vanilla extract, chocolate milk, frozen strawberries, bananas and pineapple. Pour into an ice cream maker and freeze according to the manufacturer's instructions.

Preheat the oven to 180°C (350°F) Gas 4.

Put the pastry on a lightly floured work surface. Roll out to a 3-mm/⅛-inch thickness. Using the cookie cutter, cut out 24 pastry rounds and return to the fridge to chill for 5–10 minutes. Prick the pastry rounds with a fork and fit into the tartlet pan. Chill in the fridge for a further 5–10 minutes. Once the pastry is cold, bake in the preheated oven for 25–30 minutes, or until the crust is crisp. Set aside to cool.

Spread 1 teaspoon of melted chocolate over the bottom of each cooled pie shell (reserving a little to decorate). Cover with 1 tablespoon of ice cream and put the filled shells back in the freezer for 10–20 minutes, or until frozen. When ready to serve, spoon the whipped cream into a piping bag and pipe a swirl on each pie. Top with a piece of banana and a cherry. Sprinkle with chopped nuts and drizzle with melted chocolate. Assemble on upright pie pop holders and serve immediately.

SAVORY PIES

SPINACH AND FETA PIE POPS

These savory pie pops have all the classic flavors of the Greek islands — from feta to lemon and dill. The filo pastry gives them a delicious crunch but it is quite delicate so be sure to handle them carefully while inserting the pop sticks. They make perfect canapés for any drinks party and can be enjoyed as they are or served with a refreshing yogurt and cucumber 'tzatziki' dip.

450 g/1 lb. filo/phyllo pastry sheets

60 g/4 tablespoons butter, melted

SPINACH AND FETA FILLING:

1 tablespoon olive oil

100 g/1½ cups chopped leeks

1 small onion, chopped

1 x 280-g/10-oz. package chopped, frozen spinach, thawed and well drained (squeeze out any excess moisture with hands)

2 tablespoons chopped fresh dill

2 eggs, lightly beaten

200 g/1½ cups crumbled feta

freshly squeezed juice of ½ a lemon

salt and freshly ground black pepper, to taste

TO SERVE:

a handful of mint leaves

tzatziki, for dipping

32 cake pop sticks

a baking sheet, greased

MAKES 32

Preheat the oven to 180°C (350°F) Gas 4.

To make the filling, put the olive oil in a large frying pan/skillet and add the leeks and the onion. Cook over medium heat for about 7 minutes until translucent, stirring occasionally. Stir in the spinach and add salt and pepper to taste. Remove from the heat and stir in the dill. Set aside to cool.

Put the eggs, feta, lemon juice and cooled leek and spinach mixture in a bowl and mix to combine. Set aside.

Unroll the sheets of filo pastry onto a floured work surface and keep covered with parchment paper and a damp kitchen towel to prevent drying out. Using a sharp knife, cut all the filo into 7.5 x 28-cm/3 x 11-inch strips and re-cover.

Take one strip of filo and brush with melted butter. Put 1 generous teaspoon of spinach filling 2.5 cm/1 inch from the end of the pastry strip. Very delicately, fold the end over the filling to form a triangle, then continue to fold and enclose the filling until you have a triangular parcel. When you get towards the final folds, insert the pie pop stick into the pie along the longest edge of the triangle and continue to fold over. Continue with remaining strips of filo, placing filled pies on the baking sheet and keeping them covered with a damp kitchen towel until ready to bake.

Brush all the pies lightly with melted butter and bake in the preheated oven for 20–25 minutes, or until crisp and golden brown. Scatter with mint leaves and serve warm with tzatziki for dipping.

CHICKEN POT PIE POPS

These cute pie pops have all the much-loved flavors of the classic family favorite — chicken, vegetables and a creamy bechamel sauce. For a more substantial (but still mini) version of this classic pie, spoon a more generous helping of filling into pastry shells, pressed into a mini muffin pan, and let it bubble and bake its way to becoming the ultimate comforting savory treat.

2 quantities Shortcrust Pastry (p.8), omitting the sugar

1 egg, beaten, mixed with 30 ml/ 2 tablespoons milk for egg wash

CHICKEN FILLING:

450 g/1 lb. boneless, skinless chicken breasts cut into chunks

130 g/1 cup sliced carrots

130 g/1 cup frozen peas

65 g/½ cup sliced celery

900 ml/4 cups chicken stock

50 g/3 tablespoons plus 1 teaspoon butter

1 small onion, sliced

80 g/⅔ cup plain/all-purpose flour

1-1½ teaspoons salt

¼ teaspoon ground black pepper

¼ teaspoon dried dill

320 ml/1⅓ cups milk

a 7.5-cm/3-inch fluted round cookie cutter

24 cake pop sticks

a chicken-shaped mini cookie cutter (optional)

MAKES 24

To make the filling, put the chicken, carrots, peas, celery and chicken stock in a large saucepan. Bring to a boil and cook for 15 minutes then remove from the heat.

Melt the butter in a frying pan/skillet and add the onion. Cook for 4 minutes, or until translucent. Turn the heat down to low and add the flour, salt, pepper and dill and stir to form a paste. Add the milk and stir over medium heat until the mixture is smooth. Add to the chicken mixture and stir well to combine. Return the pan to the heat and bring to the boil. Simmer for about 10 minutes, or until thick. Set aside to cool.

Put the pastry on a floured work surface and roll out to a 3-mm/⅛-inch thickness. Stamp out 48 pastry rounds using the cookie cutter and put in the fridge to chill.

Preheat the oven to 190°C (375°F) Gas 5.

Take the pastry rounds from the fridge, coat with egg wash and lay on a baking sheet 2.5 cm/1 inch apart. Put a pop cake stick in the middle of half of the pastry rounds, then add 1–2 tablespoons of filling. Top each with another pastry round and seal the edges of the pies by crimping the pastry with the tines of a fork. Re-roll any pastry trimmings to a 3-mm/⅛-inch thickness and use to stamp out 24 mini chicken shapes to decorate, if liked. Cut slits in the pies, top with the shapes, if using, and brush all the pies with egg wash. Bake in the middle of the preheated oven for 25–30 minutes, or until golden brown. Take care when serving as the filling will be hot.

QUICHE LORRAINE POPS

Although quiche is considered a typically French dish, savory egg custard pies that were mixed with vegetables actually originated as early as the 14th century in English cuisine. These pop quiches are great to serve as part of a cold finger buffet.

I quantity Shortcrust Pastry (p.8), replacing the sugar with I teaspoon dried mixed herbs

QUICHE FILLING:

I tablespoon vegetable oil

I large onion, diced

I garlic clove, finely chopped

280 g/¾ lb. cooked bacon, finely chopped

3 eggs

135 ml/½ cup plus I tablespoon double/heavy cream

260 ml/I cup plus 2 tablespoons sour cream

a pinch of ground nutmeg

¼ teaspoon ground black pepper

½ teaspoon salt

125 g/I cup grated Swiss cheese, such as Gruyère

a 7.5-cm/3-inch round cookie cutter

a 24-hole mini tartlet pan, greased

a baking sheet, lined with baking parchment

24 x wooden cooking paddle skewers or cake pop sticks

MAKES 24

Put the pastry on a floured work surface and roll out to a 3-mm/⅛-inch thickness. Stamp out 24 pastry rounds using the cookie cutter and put in the fridge to chill for 5–10 minutes. Fit the pastry rounds into the tartlet pan and prick with a fork. Put them in the freezer while you prepare the filling.

Preheat the oven to 180°C (350°F) Gas 4.

To make the filling, heat the oil in a frying pan/skillet and cook the onions for 3–4 minutes, until translucent. Add the garlic and cook for 1 minute. Remove from the heat and mix in the bacon, reserving 2 tablespoons of bacon for garnish. Set aside to cool. Using a hand-held whisk, beat the eggs, cream, sour cream, nutmeg, salt and pepper until well combined.

Remove the tartlet pan from the freezer. Put 1–2 tablespoons of the bacon mixture into each pie shell. Fill each one with egg mixture until three quarters full. Top with grated cheese and bake in the middle of the preheated oven for 12–15 minutes, or until the pastry is golden brown and the filling puffy and set in the middle. Set aside to cool, then turn the quiches out onto a lined baking sheet.

Make a small horizontal slit in the side of each quiche by poking the tip of a sharp knife into the pastry shell. Slowly insert a wooden paddle skewer into each slit then put the quiches in the fridge for at least 2 hours, until set firm. Garnish the tops of the quiches with the reserved bacon before serving cold or at room temperature.

MINI PORK PIE POPS

During the days of stagecoaches, English pork pies were a popular treat because of their sturdiness. Traditional pork pies were quite large and substantial with most weighing between one and five pounds! These cute piggies are perfect for serving as eyecatching canapés.

TRADITIONAL LARD PASTRY:

450 g/4½ cups plain/all-purpose flour

½ teaspoon salt

225 g/1 cup lard, cubed and chilled

1 egg, lightly beaten

1 egg, beaten, mixed with 30 ml/2 tablespoons milk for egg wash

PORK FILLING:

1 tablespoon olive oil

1 small onion, finely diced

3 garlic cloves, finely chopped

2 small carrots, diced

680 g/1½ lbs. minced/ground pork

450 g/1 lb. bacon, diced

1 tablespoon salt

½ teaspoon each white pepper, mace and ground nutmeg

6 black peppercorns, ground

1 teaspoon fresh thyme leaves

130 ml/½ cup chicken stock

a 7.5-cm/3-inch pig-shaped cookie cutter

24 cake pop sticks

a baking sheet, greased

MAKES 24

To make the pastry, put the flour and salt in a food processor and pulse to incorporate. Add the lard and mix on high for 10 seconds, or until the mixture resembles cornmeal. Add the egg to the mixture and combine again by pulsing the food processor for 20–30 seconds, until the mixture just starts to come together. It should be sticking together, not crumbly. Add a little water, if needed. Wrap the pastry with clingfilm/plastic wrap and chill in the fridge for at least 30 minutes.

To make the filling, heat the oil in a saucepan set over medium heat. Add the onion, garlic and carrots, and sauté for about 5 minutes, or until the onion is translucent. Set aside to cool. When cool, put the onion mixture in a bowl with the pork and bacon, salt, pepper, spices, ground peppercorns and thyme and mix well. Add the stock, 60 ml/¼ cup at a time. Cover and chill in the fridge until needed.

Preheat the oven to 180°C (350°F) Gas 4.

Put the pastry on a floured work surface and roll out to a 3-mm/⅛-inch thickness. Stamp out 48 pastry shapes using the cookie cutter and put in the fridge to chill.

Remove the pastry shapes from the fridge and lay out on a greased baking sheet, spaced 2.5 cm/1 inch apart. Paint the rims of 24 shapes with egg wash, then put a cake pop stick in the middle of each one. Top with 1–1½ tablespoons of the pork filling, 1.5 cm/½ inch from the edges of the pastry. Top with another pastry shape, press the edges gently to seal and coat with egg wash. Bake in the middle of the preheated oven for 15 minutes, then lower the temperature to 160°C (325°F) Gas 3. Bake for 30 minutes more, or until golden brown. Take care when serving as the filling will be hot.

VEGGIE PASTY POPS

Veggie pasty pops have all the richness of a meat pie with a vegetarian-friendly mushroom and cheese filling. Put these empanada-shaped snacks in kids' lunch boxes for a fun lunchtime treat, add them to your picnic hamper, or serve any time of day as a tasty and nutritious snack.

1 quantity Shortcrust Pastry (p.8), excluding the sugar

1 egg, beaten, mixed with 30 ml/ 2 tablespoons milk for egg wash

sesame seeds, for sprinkling

VEGGIE FILLING:

1 tablespoon olive oil

260 g/2 cups chopped mushrooms

1 small onion, chopped

1 tablespoon crushed garlic

1 egg

40 g/½ cup grated Cheddar

30 g/2 tablespoons butter

30 g/2 tablespoons plain/ all-purpose flour

310 ml/1¼ cups cold milk

salt and freshly ground black pepper

a 7.5-cm/3-inch round cookie cutter

a mini star-shaped cookie cutter (optional)

24 cake pop sticks

MAKES 24

Put the pastry on a floured work surface and roll out to a 3-mm/⅛-inch thickness. Stamp out 24 pastry rounds using the cookie cutter. Stamp out a small star shape on one side of each round, if liked. Put in the fridge to chill for about 5–10 minutes.

To make the veggie filling, heat the oil in a large frying pan/skillet set over medium heat. Add the mushrooms, onion and garlic and cook for 3–5 minutes, or until the onion is translucent and the mushrooms are almost thoroughly cooked. Break the egg into the pan and stir it into the mixture until cooked. Stir in the cheese. Remove from the heat and set aside until needed.

Melt the butter in a small saucepan set over medium heat. Stir in the flour to form a paste. Add the milk and stir continuously until the mixture is thick, smooth and free of lumps. Set aside to cool. When cool, mix about 120 ml/½ cup of this sauce mixture into the mushroom and cheese mixture. Add a little more to loosen the mixture. Any left over can be frozen.

Preheat the oven to 180°C (350°F) Gas 4.

Take the pastry rounds from the fridge, coat with egg wash and lay out on a baking sheet 2.5 cm/1 inch apart. Put a cake pop stick in the middle of each pastry round, then put 1–2 tablespoons of the filling onto the right-hand half of each pastry round. Fold the pastry in the middle and bring the left-hand half of each pastry round over the right to form a semi-circle. Press gently to seal the edges of the pies. Brush all the pies with egg wash and sprinkle with sesame seeds. Bake in the middle of the preheated oven for 15-20 minutes, or until crisp and golden brown. Serve hot or at room temperature.

INDEX

A

Alaska pies, sundae 48
apples: apple and Brie
   turnover pops 31
   apple pie pops 28
   mini tarte Tatin pops
   32

B

bacon: quiche Lorraine
   pops 59
bananas: banana cream
   pie pops 16
   banana-split ice cream
   pie pops 52
blueberry pie pops 19
Boston cream pie pops 35
butterscotch pecan pie
   pops 8

C

caramel: banana cream
   pie pops 16
   caramel marshmallow
   pie pops 40
   chocolate turtle pie
   pops 43
carrots: chicken pot pie
   pops 56
cheese: apple and Brie
   turnover pops 31
   quiche Lorraine pops
   59
   spinach and feta pie
   pops 55
   veggie pasty pops 63
cheesecake pie pops,
   chocolate cherry 47
cherries: Boston cream
   pie pops 35
   cherry pie pops 27
   chocolate cherry
   cheesecake pie pops
chicken pot pie pops 56
chocolate: banana-split
   ice cream pie pops 52

Boston cream pie pops
   35
   chocolate and peanut
   butter pie pops 36
   chocolate cherry
   cheesecake pie pops
   47
   chocolate-dipped Key
   lime pie pops 44
   chocolate pastry 15
   chocolate pudding pie
   pops 39
   chocolate turtle pie
   pops 43
   orangesicle ice cream
   pie pops 51
coconut cream pie pops
   15
cream: banana cream pie
   pops 16
   Boston cream pie pops
   35

F

filo (phyllo) pastry:
   spinach and feta pie
   pops 55

I

ice cream: banana-split
   ice cream pie pops 52
   chocolate-dipped Key
   lime pie pops 44
   orangesicle ice cream
   pie pops 51
   sundae Alaska pies 48

K

Key lime pie pops,
   chocolate-dipped 44

L

lard pastry 60
lattice crust 8
leeks: spinach and feta
   pie pops 55

lemon: lemon meringue
   pie pops 11
   Shaker lemon pie pops
   24
   sundae Alaska pies 48
lime: chocolate-dipped
   Key lime pie pops
   44

M

marshmallows: caramel
   marshmallow pie pops
   40
meringue: lemon
   meringue pie pops 11
   sundae Alaska pies 48
mini pork pie pops 60
mini tarte Tatin pops 32
mushrooms: veggie pasty
   pops 63

N

nectarine and peach
   brown sugar pie pops
   20

O

orangesicle ice cream pie
   pops 51

P

pastry: chocolate pastry 15
   pop tart pastry 23
   rich sweet pastry 12
   shortcrust pastry 8
   traditional lard pastry
   60
pastry cream, vanilla 15
peaches: nectarine and
   peach brown sugar pie
   pops 20
peanut butter: chocolate
   and peanut butter pie
   pops 36
peas: chicken pot pie
   pops 56

pecans: butterscotch
   pecan pie pops 8
   chocolate turtle pie
   pops 43
phyllo (see filo)
pineapple: banana-split
   ice cream pie pops 52
pop tart pastry 23
pork pie pops 60
puff pastry: apple and
   Brie turnover pops 31
   mini tarte Tatin pops
   32
pumpkin pie pops 12

Q

quiche Lorraine pops 59

R

rich sweet pastry 12

S

Shaker lemon pie pops
   24
shortcrust pastry 8
sorbet, lemon 48
spinach and feta pie pops
   55
strawberries: banana-
   split ice cream pie
   pops 52
   strawberry pop tart pops
   23
   sundae Alaska pies 48
sundae Alaska pies 48

V

vanilla pastry cream 15
veggie pasty pops 63